GREEN BOND MARKET SURVEY FOR INDONESIA

INSIGHTS ON THE PERSPECTIVES OF INSTITUTIONAL INVESTORS AND UNDERWRITERS

NOVEMBER 2022

ASIAN DEVELOPMENT BANK

© 2022 Asian Development Bank
6 ADB Avenue, Mandaluyong City, 1550 Metro Manila, Philippines
Tel +63 2 8632 4444; Fax +63 2 8636 2444
www.adb.org

Some rights reserved. Published in 2022.

ISBN 978-92-9269-894-2 (print); 978-92-9269-895-9 (electronic); 978-92-9269-896-6 (ebook)
Publication Stock No. TCS220536-2
DOI: http://dx.doi.org/10.22617/TCS220536-2

CONTENTS

TABLE, FIGURES, AND BOXES

BOXES

ACKNOWLEDGMENTS

The lead authors—Kosintr Puongsophol, Cedric Rimaud, Oth Marulou Gagni, and Alita Lestor, all from the Economic Research and Regional Cooperation Department (ERCD) of the Asian Development Bank—would like to particularly thank Satoru Yamadera, advisor, ERCD, and Richard Supangan, senior economics officer, ERCD for their support and contributions. Editing by Kevin Donahue. Design and layout by Prince Nicdao.

The lead authors would also like to thank the Global Green Growth Institute team—comprising Srinath Komarina, Hien Tran, Thinh Tran, Minh Tran, and Ha Nguyen—for their inputs and suggestions.

We would like to express our appreciation to the United Nations Development Programme team—led by Muhammad Didi Hardiana, Ralista Haroen, Nila Murti, Achmad Nasution, and Garnadipa Gilang, all from United Nations Development Programme Indonesia—for their support and contributions.

Finally, we would like to express our heartfelt gratitude to the Financial Services Authority, the Indonesia Stock Exchange, and local industry associations, as well as to all respondents for their assistance with and participation in the survey.

ABBREVIATIONS

ABMI   ASEAN+3 Asian Bond Markets Initiative

ADB   Asian Development Bank

ASEAN   Association of Southeast Asian Nations

ASEAN+3   ASEAN plus the People's Republic of China, Japan, and the Republic of Korea

ESG   environmental, social, and governance

GSS   green, social, and sustainability

OJK   Otoritas Jasa Keuangan (Financial Services Authority)

SDG   Sustainable Development Goal

USD   United States dollar

SUMMARY AND KEY FINDINGS

SURVEY HIGHLIGHTS

▷ The survey was conducted in March 2022 via an online platform and received a total of 154 responses from 108 local institutional investors, mainly comprising pension funds, insurance companies, and asset management companies; 6 local underwriters and rating agencies; and 40 securities issuers.

▷ While most local institutional investors expressed interest in investing in green bonds, a substantial proportion of respondents indicated that they lack the resources and capacity to develop and implement environmental, social, and governance (ESG) investment policies. In the meantime, all underwriters indicated that they are willing to explore the possibility of underwriting green bonds for their clients. However, almost half of issuers responded that they are not yet interested in issuing green bonds, but with a majority of respondents indicating an interest in issuing green bonds in the next 3 years.

▷ Renewable energy, energy efficiency, and clean transportation were regarded as the most promising sectors for green bond market growth in Indonesia among all respondents. Underwriters identified green buildings as another promising sector in terms of potential issuance.

▷ A majority of investors cited a lack of a green project pipeline as a major impediment to the development of the green bond market in Indonesia. Meanwhile, most underwriters mentioned a lack of awareness of green bonds and not understanding their clear benefits as the two primary barriers. While issuers agree that a lack of knowledge is a major impediment, they also stated that the additional procedures required to issue a green bond, as well as the additional issuance costs, are significant disadvantages.

▷ A majority of investors believe that greater policy clarity from the government and regulators is critical for the development of the green bond market, followed by tax incentives for green bond issuers and investors. Underwriters believe that preferential buying by institutional investors and an increased pipeline of green projects are critical to increasing the green bond supply in Indonesia. Tax incentives and policy clarity from the government are also important, according to issuers.

The green bond market in Indonesia has the potential to expand further. The majority of respondents are interested in green bonds but lack the necessary resources and capacities to invest in or issue green bonds. While a significant number of green bonds have been issued in offshore markets, Indonesia has enormous potential to develop a domestic green bond market denominated in the local currency, given the strong interest among domestic capital market stakeholders.*

Renewable energy, energy efficiency, clean transportation, and green buildings are considered the sectors with the most potential. Investors and underwriters identified renewable energy, energy efficiency, clean transportation, and green buildings as the main sectors that can drive green bond market growth in Indonesia (**Table**). Meanwhile, a majority of local investors are already investing in ESG indices that comprise companies with an outstanding ESG performance (**Box 1**).

Table: Most Promising Sectors for Green Bonds in Indonesia
(share of respondents indicating agreement, %)

Investors			Underwriters		
Renewable Energy	Clean Transportation	Energy Efficiency	Renewable Energy	Energy Efficiency and Green Buildings	Clean Transportation
23	17	16	33	20	13

Source: Authors' compilation based on survey results.

The benefits of green bond issuance must be more clearly articulated. There is still a relatively high share of potential issuers that remain unconvinced of the benefits of green bonds. In particular, there appears to be a lack of awareness of green and other thematic bonds, a lack of knowledge of the regulatory advances made by the Financial Services Authority (OJK) to spur the market, as well as a belief that green bonds do not carry substantial benefits. The market appears to be waiting for more concrete incentives such as subsidies or tax benefits. In terms of timing, a large portion of the market appears to think that the issuance of green bonds is a medium-term objective, not an immediate one. The majority of investors cited the absence of a pipeline of green projects as a significant barrier to the development of the green bond market in Indonesia. To meet the increasing demand of investors, it is necessary to increase the supply of domestic green bonds, and this is an area where development partners could play a role.

There is an urgent need for more capacity building among advisors, underwriters, and potential issuers. A large portion of market practitioners indicate that they lack awareness and knowledge of the green bond market. They also recognize that the issuance of thematic bonds is more complex than conventional bonds and that they do not yield substantial added benefits.

---

*   Climate Bonds Initiative. 2021. *ASEAN Sustainable Finance Market 2021*. London.

Greater policy clarity from the government and regulators is needed. A majority of investors believe that greater policy clarity from governments and regulators is necessary for the growth of the green bond market, like for example some guidelines for issuers and investors on the definition of thematic bond issuance, as well as some indication of what support governments and regulators can provide to the market. This could be why there is not yet a sufficient supply of green bonds in the local market. Meanwhile, underwriters believe that preferential purchasing by institutional investors could be a significant factor in getting potential issuers to consider a green bond issuance. If there is no obvious demand for green bonds, issuers may be hesitant to sell them. From the perspective of issuers, government tax incentives and policy clarity are also essential.

INTRODUCTION

Background and Objective

The Asian Development Bank (ADB) is collaborating closely with the Association of Southeast Asian Nations (ASEAN), the People's Republic of China, Japan, and the Republic of Korea—collectively known as ASEAN+3—to promote the development of local currency bond markets and regional bond market integration through the Asian Bond Markets Initiative (ABMI). The ABMI was established in 2002 to bolster the resilience of ASEAN+3 financial systems by developing local currency bond markets as an alternative source to foreign-currency-denominated, short-term bank loans for long-term investment financing.

ADB, as Secretariat for the ABMI, is implementing a regional technical assistance program to promote sustainable local currency bond market development with support from the People's Republic of China Poverty Reduction and Regional Cooperation Fund. This technical assistance was developed and is being implemented with guidance from ASEAN+3 finance ministers and central bank governors, and in accordance with the ABMI Medium-Term Road Map for 2019–2022.

This survey report, conducted in collaboration with the Global Green Growth Institute, aims to assess institutional investors' interest in green bonds issued in Indonesia, as well as the perspectives of local arrangers and underwriters on their clients' interest in green bond issuance. The survey assessed market drivers, impediments, and development priorities for Indonesia's sustainable finance market to assist development partners in identifying potential areas of support to accelerate the development of Indonesia's sustainable finance market.

Methodologies

In March 2022, ADB and the Global Green Growth Institute conducted the survey via an online platform and received a total of 154 responses from 108 local institutional investors, mainly comprising pension funds, insurance companies, and asset management companies; 6 local underwriters and rating agencies; and 40 securities issuers.

OVERVIEW OF THE INDONESIAN SUSTAINABLE BOND MARKET

Indonesia's sustainable bond market has been supported by the strong commitment of the government and the issuance of eight sovereign green *sukuk* (Islamic bonds) since 2018, both in the offshore and onshore markets; well-developed green, social, and sustainability (GSS) and Sustainable Development Goal (SDG) bond frameworks; and the active role played by the Financial Services Authority (OJK). Outside of the sovereign issuances, other sustainability bond issuances include those by both financial and nonfinancial corporates. This has made Indonesia the second-largest green finance market in the ASEAN region.

The total outstanding amount of GSS bonds in Indonesia was approximately USD7.0 billion at the end of March 2022, with public sector issuances leading the way (**Figure 1**).

Green bonds are the most common type of sustainable bond in the Indonesian market, followed by sustainability bonds and sustainability-linked bonds (**Figure 2**). The majority of green bonds in the Indonesian market have been issued by the central government and other state-owned enterprises. Private sector entities, including financial institutions, have also issued green bonds for renewable energy projects and nature-based solutions.

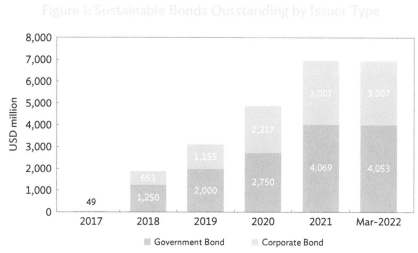

Figure 1: Sustainable Bonds Outstanding by Issuer Type

USD = United States dollar.
Note: All data as of 26 July 2022. Data were obtained using Bloomberg LP's SRCH function. The SRCH criteria included green bonds, social bonds, sustainability bonds, sustainability-linked bonds, and transition bonds.
Sources: *AsianBondsOnline* and Bloomberg LP.

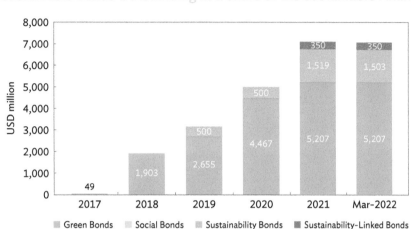

Figure 2: Sustainable Bonds Outstanding as a Share of the Sustainable Finance Market

USD = United States dollar.
Note: All data as of 26 July 2022. Data were obtained using Bloomberg LP's SRCH function. The SRCH criteria included green bonds, social bonds, sustainability bonds, sustainability-linked bonds, and transition bonds.
Sources: *AsianBondsOnline* and Bloomberg LP.

The sustainability bond market in Indonesia emerged following the issuance of a USD500 million sustainability bond by Bank Rakyat Indonesia in March 2019. The bond, with a coupon of 3.95%, was very successful, attracting a demand that was 8.2 times the size of the offer. The proceeds were targeted at social projects (e.g., affordable basic infrastructure, access to essential services, affordable housing, employment generation, and socioeconomic advancement and empowerment), as well as environmental projects (e.g., renewable energy, green buildings, pollution prevention and control, environmentally sustainable management of living natural resources and land use, clean transportation, sustainable water, and wastewater management). This was followed in 2021 by issuances from Bank Mandiri (USD300 million), PT Indonesia Infrastructure Finance (USD150 million), and the Government of Indonesia (EUR500 million).

The first sustainability-linked bond was issued by PT Japfa Comfeed Indonesia Tbk. in March 2021. The bond, which was listed on the Singapore Stock Exchange, was also the first environmentally friendly USD-denominated bond in the agri-food industry in Southeast Asia.[1]

In terms of currency, almost all sustainable bonds from Indonesian issuers were issued in offshore markets in US dollars (**Figure 3**). Only around 0.25% of outstanding sustainable bonds have been issued in Indonesian rupiah. This demonstrates the importance of the foreign currency bond market in attracting offshore capital for the financing of projects by domestic corporations and in meeting the government's need to raise funds, particularly as the country seeks to achieve the SDGs in the aftermath of the coronavirus disease pandemic.

---

[1] *IDN Financials*. 2021. Japfa Issues a Sustainability-Linked Bond Worth USD350 Million. 19 March.

Figure 3: Issuance Currency of Sustainable Bonds Outstanding

0.25%

99.75%

■ FCY Bonds   ■ LCY Bonds

FCY = foreign currency, LCY = local currency.
Notes: All data as of 26 July 2022. Data were obtained using Bloomberg LP's SRCH function. The SRCH criteria included green bonds, social bonds, sustainability bonds, sustainability-linked bonds, and transition bonds.
Sources: *AsianBondsOnline* and Bloomberg LP.

In 2021, the volume of sustainability bonds issued (USD1.03 billion) surpassed the volume of green bonds issued (USD750 million) for the first time (**Figure 4**). It is notable that no Indonesian entity has issued a social bond. This may be due to the fact that issuers prefer sustainability bonds in which bond proceeds can be allocated to both green and social projects, allowing issuers more flexibility. In addition, corporate issuers may believe that social projects are not bankable, thus the social bond market's development should initially be driven by the government.

Figure 4: Annual Issuance of Sustainable Bonds by Bond Type

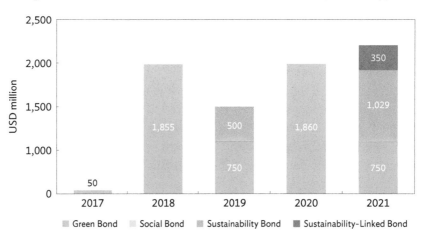

■ Green Bond   ■ Social Bond   ■ Sustainability Bond   ■ Sustainability-Linked Bond

USD = United States dollar.
Note: All data as of 26 July 2022. Data were obtained using Bloomberg LP's SRCH function. The SRCH criteria included green bonds, social bonds, sustainability bonds, sustainability-linked bonds, and transition bonds.
Sources: *AsianBondsOnline* and Bloomberg LP.

RECENT INITIATIVES IN SUSTAINABLE FINANCE

Indonesia started its sustainable finance journey in 2017 with the implementation of the Sustainable Finance Roadmap in Indonesia, 2015–2019 (Phase I).[2] According to POJK 51/POJK.03/2017 on the Implementation of Sustainable Finance and Circular Letter No. 16/SEOJK04/2021 on the Format and Contents of Annual Report, financial services companies, issuers, and public companies must implement sustainable finance and submit to the OJK a sustainable finance action plan and a sustainable report. Specific guidelines were issued to help them implement the new regulations. In 2017, the OJK also issued Regulation No. 60/POJK.04/2017 to provide guidance on the issuance process and terms for green bonds, making Indonesia among the first countries in ASEAN to issue a green bond regulation. In addition, the Ministry of Finance and the OJK jointly drafted a National Strategy for Financial Market Development, 2018–2024 to create a more active financial market, including GSS instruments.

The coronavirus disease pandemic created new challenges to the development of the financial service sector. In December 2020, the OJK released the Indonesian Financial Services Sector Master Plan, 2021–2025, building on Phase I of the Sustainable Finance Roadmap. Included in the master plan was a focus on sustainable finance toward the achievement of the SDGs. New initiatives are expected to be launched soon to create a more vibrant sustainable finance market. Among them, a sustainable finance taxonomy is needed to further clarify the types of financing that would fall in that category.

Phase I of the Sustainable Finance Roadmap was followed in early 2021 by the Sustainable Finance Roadmap in Indonesia, 2021–2025 (Phase II).[3] Its objective is to develop new incentives and harmonize regulations.

On the supply side, the roadmap seeks to increase the resilience and competitiveness of financial institutions, raise their contributions to the attainment of the SDGs and climate change resilience, enhance their capacity, and improve their literacy in the field of sustainable finance.

On the demand side, the roadmap aims to increase demand for sustainable products, support industries offering sustainable products, and develop a certification scheme for sustainable products and related professions. Other notable additions to Phase II of the Sustainable Finance Roadmap included new plans to further develop the sustainable finance ecosystem, raise awareness among financial services firms, and support the development of the necessary skill set.

---

[2] OJK. 2015. *Sustainable Finance Roadmap in Indonesia, 2015–2019*. Jakarta.

[3] OJK. 2021. *Sustainable Finance Roadmap in Indonesia, 2021–2025*. Jakarta.

The issuance of sovereign green bonds and an SDG bond signaled the strong commitment of the government to using labeled instruments as part of its national financing strategy. Some of the government's green *sukuk* issuances have gained international recognition and the response from investors exceeded the usual demand for Indonesian government securities (**Box 1**).

A dedicated website was launched to support the implementation of environmental, social, and governance (ESG) policies across Indonesian financial institutions.[4] Four local green indices were created to signal ESG leaders among Indonesian listed companies. In 2021, the Indonesian Stock Exchange came out publicly in support of the Taskforce for Climate-Related Financial Disclosures, which breaks down climate-related risks into acute and chronic risks, and identifies four primary transition risks: policy and regulatory, market and economic, technology, and reputational.

In January 2022, the Indonesia Green Taxonomy 1.0 was launched by the OJK. It was a significant milestone in defining categories that are eligible for green financing for all stakeholders carrying out sustainable economic activities. It also represented a significant effort to encourage the private sector to comply with ESG regulations and prioritize green investments.

In its current form, the taxonomy includes 919 sectors mapped into subsectors, groups, and business activities aligned with Level 5 of the Indonesian Standard for Industrial Classification, which is the most specific level of Indonesia's Central Bureau Statistics. Three categories are included: (i) green, (ii) yellow, and (iii) red. For a subsector to qualify as "green," it must do no significant harm, apply minimum safeguards, and have a positive impact on the environment. Subsectors complying with the "do no significant harm" principle are otherwise classified as "yellow," while harmful activities are branded as "red." The 904 sectors and subsectors that were not included in the first draft of the taxonomy did not meet the government's prerequisite for green classification. Subsequently, additional publications by the OJK indicated that the other 15 sectors could meet the green category.[5]

Indonesian companies must also comply with Indonesia-specific certifications, such as the Ministry of Environment and Forestry's Greenhouse Gas Emissions Reduction Certification and its Company Performance and Management Rating Assessment Program, as well as the Ministry of Agriculture's Indonesia Sustainable Palm Oil Certification.

---

[4] ESG. ESG at a Glance. https://esg.idx.co.id.

[5] OJK. 2022. Taksonomi Hijau Indonesia Edisi. Jakarta.

Box 1: United Nations Development Programme Assistance in the Indonesian Green *Sukuk* and Sustainable Development Goal Bond Market

Indonesia first entered the thematic bond market with an inaugural issuance of green *sukuk* in 2018, which was followed by annual issuances in subsequent years, both in the global and domestic retail markets. As of May 2022, the issuance of green *sukuk* had raised an aggregate of USD5.0 billion globally, while retail green *sukuk* (first issued in 2019) had cumulatively raised USD830 million.

The United Nations Development Programme (UNDP) has enjoyed a longstanding partnership with the Government of Indonesia dating back to 2016 with the establishment of Climate Budget Tagging—a budgeting mechanism allowing the government to monitor and track its spending on climate mitigation and adaptation efforts—that later paved the way for green *sukuk* (Islamic bonds). UNDP support has been channeled through the provision of technical assistance during the development of the green bond and *sukuk* framework, an external review of the framework, project selection and evaluation in the pre-issuance process, and impact measurement and reporting for post-issuance. UNDP also contributed to public sector capacity building and institutional strengthening with regard to the overall context of green financing, as well as the transparency and disclosure requirements that follow. A series of campaign and advocacy efforts were also undertaken to further enhance the visibility of Indonesia's pioneering green *sukuk* initiative, such as through exposure in national and international forums and the development of a broad range of green *sukuk* knowledge products (e.g., handbook, studies, video) capturing Indonesia's green *sukuk* journey in global and domestic markets.

The string of successes from green *sukuk* issuances inspired the Government of Indonesia to develop Sustainable Development Goal (SDG) bonds (**Figure**), with UNDP taking an active role in this process. The provision of support commenced in 2020 with the development of a feasibility study in collaboration with the Ministry of Finance, which resulted in recommendations for the ministry to undertake steps in preparing the issuance of SDG bonds. Further, UNDP

Figure: Indonesia's Green *Sukuk* and Sustainable Development Goal Bond Issuance, 2018–2022

March 2018	1st Global Green Sukuk	**USD1.25 billion**
February 2019	2nd Global Green Sukuk	**USD750 million**
November 2019	1st Retail Green Sukuk (ST-006)	**IDR1.46 trillion**
June 2020	3rd Global Green Sukuk	**USD750 million**
November 2020	2nd Retail Green Sukuk (ST-007)	**IDR5.4 trillion**
June 2021	4th Global Green Sukuk	**USD750 million**
September 2021	1st Global SDG Bond	**EUR500 million**
November 2021	3rd Retail Green Sukuk (ST-008)	**IDR5 trillion**
May 2022	5th Global Green Sukuk	**USD1.5 billion**

EUR = euro, IDR = Indonesian rupiah, SDG = Sustainable Development Goal, USD = United States dollar.
Source: UNDP.

continued to work closely with the Ministry of Finance in developing the Government of Indonesia's SDG Securities Framework and its subsequent second-party opinion external review process.

These preparations led to Indonesia's inaugural SDG bond issuance in the global capital market in September 2021. This 12-year EUR500 million bond met with a positive reception, leading to a 2.4x oversubscription. UNDP provided support during the project evaluation and selection process to ensure that proceeds were allocated toward SDG achievement efforts. Close collaboration was also maintained for the development of the Government of Indonesia's first annual *SDG Bond Allocation and Impact Report*. The government is also expected to issue its *SDG Bond and Blue Bond and Sukuk Report*, and UNDP remains ready to provide its utmost support to ensure yet another success story.

Source: UNDP.

SURVEY RESULTS

The survey was conducted in March 2022 among 108 local institutional investors (fund managers, financial institutions, insurance companies) and local underwriters and advisors. A summary of the survey's findings is given below.

Institutional Investors

The survey began by asking respondents about their firms' interest and/or current investment in green financial instruments. The vast majority of respondents indicated that they were interested in investing, but they had limited awareness and resources. Others are either not interested in green financial instruments at this stage or,

if they were, their respective firms are currently developing an action plan (**Figure 5**). Only a few respondents were already mandated to invest in green bonds as part of their overall investment mandate.

Due to the fact that most respondents either have limited awareness and resources or are still developing an action plan, the vast majority of respondents also indicated that green bonds comprised less than 5% of their aggregate portfolios. Green investments comprised between 21% and 30% of portfolios for only 1% of all respondents, while 5% of respondents, primarily pension funds, indicated that green investments comprised more than 30% of their portfolios (**Figure 6**).

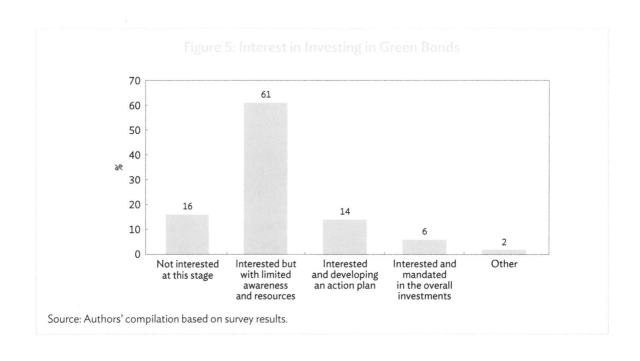

Figure 5: Interest in Investing in Green Bonds

Source: Authors' compilation based on survey results.

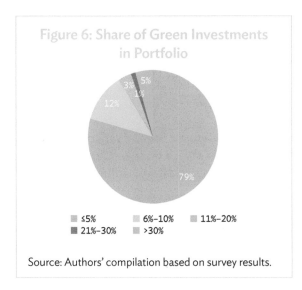

Figure 6: Share of Green Investments in Portfolio

■ ≤5%   ■ 6%–10%   ■ 11%–20%
■ 21%–30%   ■ >30%

Source: Authors' compilation based on survey results.

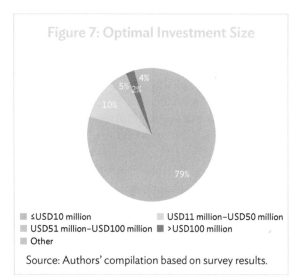

Figure 7: Optimal Investment Size

■ ≤USD10 million   ■ USD11 million–USD50 million
■ USD51 million–USD100 million ■ >USD100 million
■ Other

Source: Authors' compilation based on survey results.

When asked about ticket size, 79% of respondents indicated a preference for investments of less than USD10 million, while 10% indicated a willingness to invest up to USD50 million per transaction (**Figure 7**). Only 2% of respondents indicated that their optimal investment size was more than USD100 million.

In terms of sector preference, renewable energy (20%), energy efficiency (16%), and ESG indices and benchmarks (13%) are the top sectors in

respondents' investment portfolios (**Figure 8**). (For more on Indonesian ESG Indices, see **Box 2**). Meanwhile, 12% of respondents have no exposure to green investments, while only 3% of respondents have investments related to green buildings. For these investors to be able to invest in green financial instruments, additional support from development partners is required to increase their capacities.

When asked their primary reasons for investing in green bonds, the majority of investors believe

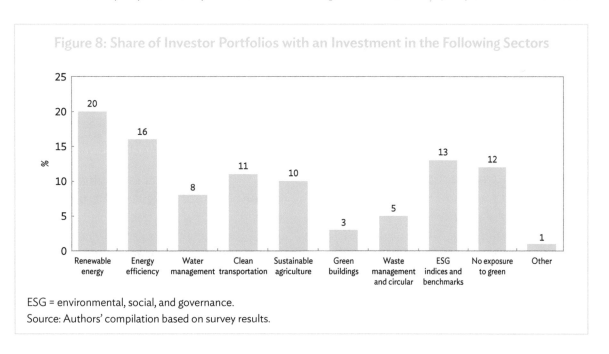

Figure 8: Share of Investor Portfolios with an Investment in the Following Sectors

ESG = environmental, social, and governance.
Source: Authors' compilation based on survey results.

Box 2: Indonesian Environmental, Social, and Governance Indices

The Indonesia Stock Exchange (IDX) recognizes the significance of environmental, social, and governance (ESG) investing to support the expansion of sustainable financing in the Indonesian capital market. The exchange has issued a regulation to support and encourage the issuance of green bonds in Indonesia through Rule Number I-B. On top

of that, the Indonesia Stock Exchange has also created four ESG-based indices, which are described below.

To learn more about companies that were indexed to these two indices, see https://www.idx.co.id/data-pasar/data-saham/indeks-saham.

IDXESGL (ESG LEADERS)	SRI-KEHATI
An index that measures the stock price of 15–30 companies that have a good ESG performance and do not have significant controversies. The index is selected from stocks with high trading liquidity that also have a good financial performance. ESG scoring and controversy analysis is conducted by Sustainalytics.	An index that measures the stock price of 25 listed companies, selected by the Indonesian Biodiversity Foundation (KEHATI Foundation), that have a good performance in encouraging sustainable businesses and raising ESG awareness, which is also known as sustainable and responsible investment (SRI). SRI-KEHATI is a jointly developed index with the KEHATI Foundation.
ESG SECTOR LEADERS IDX KEHATI	ESG QUALITY 45 IDX KEHATI
An index that offers broad market exposure and diversification by choosing representative in each industry with best ESG score. Stocks with above-average ESG scores are selected to represent their respective industries and grouped by IDX Industry Classification. This index is jointly developed with the KEHATI Foundation.	An index that measures the stock price of 45 companies that consider the quality of financial and ESG aspects with relatively large market capitalization and high liquidity. This index is jointly developed with the KEHATI Foundation.

Source: Indonesia Stock Exchange. *ESG Investments*. Jakarta.

that this would give them an opportunity to diversify their institution's investment portfolio (**Figure 9**). Nearly 90% of respondents also cited increased transparency as a reason for their interest in green bonds. This may be due to the fact that green bond issuers are required to explain in their issuance framework how proceeds from the bonds will be used, as well as to report on how proceeds have been or will be allocated to the projects listed in the framework and any potential environmental benefits. A significant number of respondents believed that investing in green bonds would enhance

their organization's green image. The majority of respondents also perceived green bonds to be more stable and liquid than conventional bonds.

While there are clear motivations for investing in green bonds, the survey asked respondents to identify any major obstacles to investing, as green investments are generally not a very significant part of their investment portfolios. A quarter of respondents stated that the primary impediment is the inadequate supply of green bonds in the domestic market (**Figure 10**). This clearly indicates that Indonesia's current

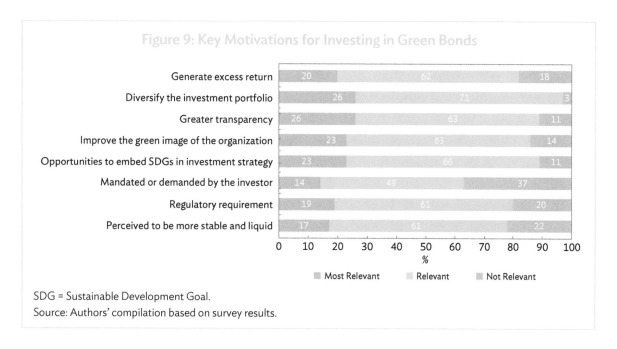

Figure 9: Key Motivations for Investing in Green Bonds

SDG = Sustainable Development Goal.
Source: Authors' compilation based on survey results.

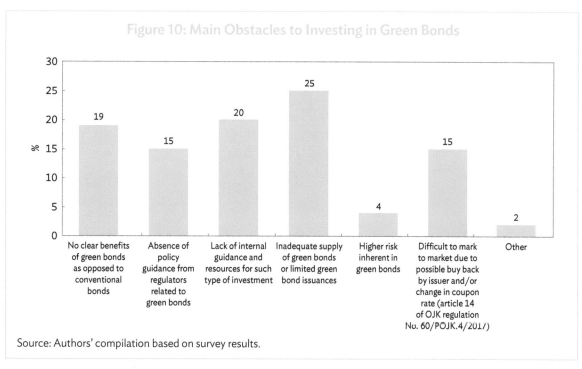

Figure 10: Main Obstacles to Investing in Green Bonds

Source: Authors' compilation based on survey results.

supply of green bonds, especially those issued domestically, are insufficient to meet demand. As a result, there is a significant opportunity for issuers to consider green bond issuance as a means of diversifying their investor base.

Around 20% of respondents also suggested that the lack of internal guidance and resources for

such types of investment is also relevant, while 19% of respondents indicated that the absence of clear benefits from investing in green bonds was one of the key inhibiting factors. Similarly, around 15% of respondents also indicated that the mandatory buyback of bonds and a possible change in the coupon rate in the event the bond no longer carries a green label could make it difficult for investors to mark to market, especially for long-term investors. Prior to the initiation of a mandatory buyback or increase in coupon rate, an issuer must prepare a plan outlining how they will ensure that the projects they are financing with proceeds from the bond are or will be aligned with environmental-based business activity, as required by OJK Regulation No. 60 /POJK.04/2017. The issuer must submit a plan to the OJK within 14 days of becoming aware that their business activity and/or other activities no longer comply with the requirements and must rectify the issue within 1 year of submitting a report to the OJK. In the event that the issuer is unable to resolve the issue, Article 14 of OJK Regulation No. 60/POJK.04/2017 permits the holders of the green bond to request that the issuer repurchase the green bond and/or increase coupon payments on the green bond.

When investing in green bonds, investors continue to prioritize credit ratings and valuation and pricing (**Figure 11**). This is unsurprising given that performance is central to a fund manager's mandate. The other most critical factor is the company profile or management team and the historical performance, as these directly correlate to the bond's operations. The next set of priorities are the ESG impact of the bond, alongside the issuance currency. Finally, brand association and alignment with non-green investment mandates score relatively low. A vast majority of investors believe that external review by a third party is highly important or important and can aid them in making investment decisions.

Respondents were requested to select up to three options that they felt could encourage the growth of Indonesia's green bond market. More than 20% of respondents recommended that the government provides regulatory support and clarity on the approaches to developing a domestic green bond market. Furthermore, respondents suggested that the introduction of tax incentives or grant schemes would entice investors to hold more green bonds (**Figure 12**). Meanwhile, nearly 15% of responses indicated that a clear taxonomy defining what constitutes green assets, projects, and expenditures, and increased ESG disclosure by listed companies, would significantly assist investors in making green investment decisions.

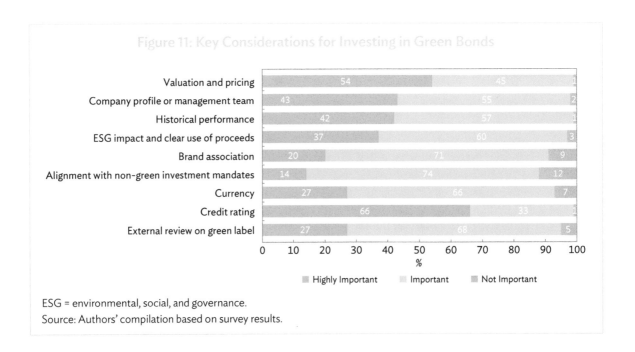

Figure 11: Key Considerations for Investing in Green Bonds

	Highly Important	Important	Not Important
Valuation and pricing	54	45	1
Company profile or management team	43	55	2
Historical performance	42	57	1
ESG impact and clear use of proceeds	37	60	3
Brand association	20	71	9
Alignment with non-green investment mandates	14	74	12
Currency	27	66	7
Credit rating	66	33	1
External review on green label	27	68	5

ESG = environmental, social, and governance.
Source: Authors' compilation based on survey results.

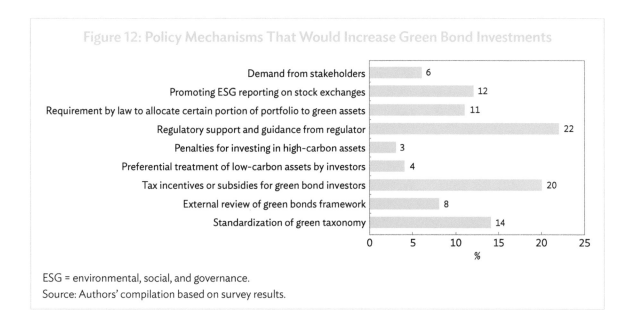

Figure 12: Policy Mechanisms That Would Increase Green Bond Investments

ESG = environmental, social, and governance.
Source: Authors' compilation based on survey results.

As mentioned above, the OJK introduced the Indonesia Green Taxonomy 1.0 in January 2022. This taxonomy will be used as (i) the basis for the development of incentive and disincentive policies by various ministries and institutions, including the OJK; and (ii) guidelines for information openness, risk management, and the development of innovative sustainable finance products and/or services. Furthermore, the development of the Indonesia Green Taxonomy 1.0 is expected to provide an overview of the classification of sectors and subsectors categorized as green to avoid greenwashing practices.[6]

An increasing number of local investors are looking for investment opportunities in green bonds. The survey investigated which types of green bond issuers respondents are interested in. Local institutional investors indicated that they are mostly interested in sovereign issuances, followed by green bonds issued by development banks. Next were financial institutions, including commercial banks, and insurance companies (**Figure 13**).

For nonfinancial institutions, almost 27% of respondents believed that issuers from the renewable energy sector offered the greatest investment opportunities, followed by 17% for the clean transportation sector (**Figure 14**). These findings are consistent with the sector breakdown of respondents' current portfolios of green assets.

On policies needed to develop the green bond market, almost all respondents emphasized the critical importance of government and regulatory policy clarity to increase the amount of investment capital allocated to this sector. Indeed, more than 50% of respondents believed this to be "most relevant." Tax incentives for green bond issuers were viewed as having nearly as important an impact on the development of the market.

Respondents believe that establishment of a centralized information platform displaying information on all green or sustainable bonds from Indonesian issuers and preferential buying by institutional investors would also provide some support for the market (**Figure 15**).

---

[6]   OJK. 2022. *Indonesia Green Taxonomy Edition 1.0.* Jakarta.

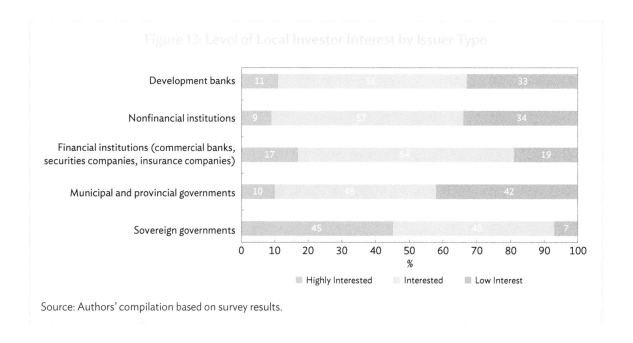

Figure 13: Level of Local Investor Interest by Issuer Type

Source: Authors' compilation based on survey results.

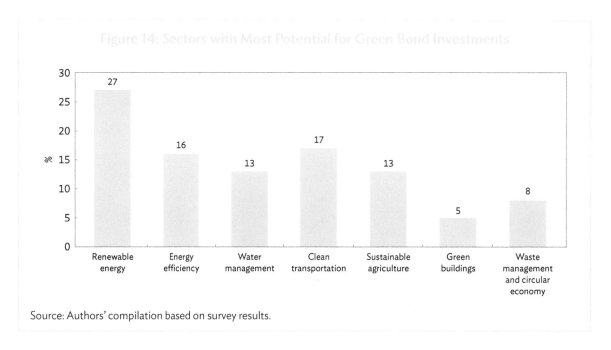

Figure 14: Sectors with Most Potential for Green Bond Investments

Source: Authors' compilation based on survey results.

Regarding capacity development, respondents were near unanimous in agreement that investors require additional training (**Figure 16**). Additionally, it was felt that chief financial officers of listed companies and deal teams should be trained to gain a better understanding of green bonds and their issuance process.

This would lead to an increase in the supply of green bonds to meet investor demand.

Among investors interested in regional investments, Singapore, Thailand, and Malaysia are the preferred investment destinations (**Figure 17**). When asked about the underlying

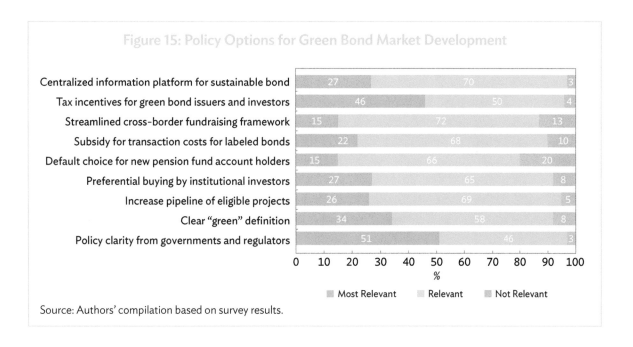

Figure 15: Policy Options for Green Bond Market Development

Source: Authors' compilation based on survey results.

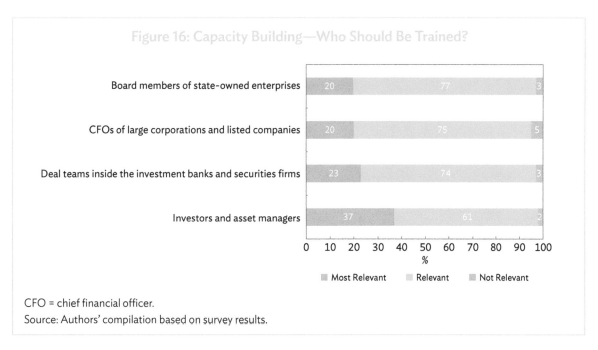

Figure 16: Capacity Building—Who Should Be Trained?

CFO = chief financial officer.
Source: Authors' compilation based on survey results.

issuance currency, 90% of respondents preferred hard currencies such as the United States dollar, Singapore dollar, euro, or Japanese yen (**Figure 18**).

Lastly, investors were asked if they would be interested in investing in other types of

thematic bonds that have the potential to further mainstream climate finance in Indonesia (**Figure 19**). For a majority of investors, SDG bonds and sustainability bonds are the two instruments in which they are most interested. This may be attributable in part to the fact that the Indonesian government issued

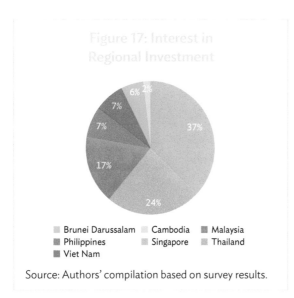

Figure 17: Interest in Regional Investment

37%
24%
17%
7%
7%
6%
2%

Brunei Darussalam Cambodia Malaysia
Philippines Singapore Thailand
Viet Nam

Source: Authors' compilation based on survey results.

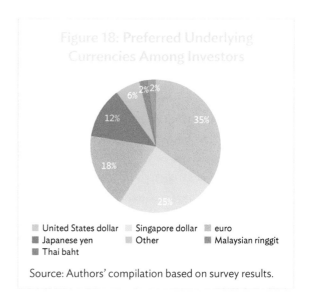

Figure 18: Preferred Underlying Currencies Among Investors

35%
25%
18%
12%
6%
2% 2%

United States dollar Singapore dollar euro
Japanese yen Other Malaysian ringgit
Thai baht

Source: Authors' compilation based on survey results.

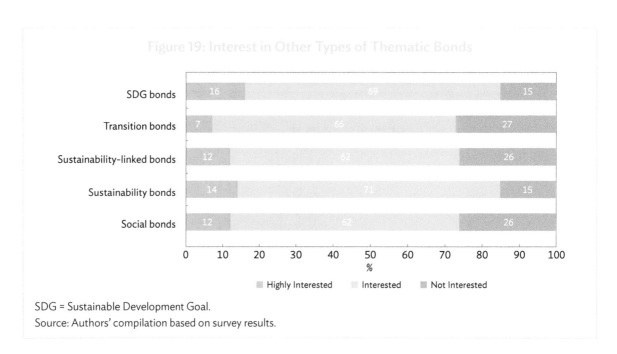

Figure 19: Interest in Other Types of Thematic Bonds

	Highly Interested	Interested	Not Interested
SDG bonds	16	69	15
Transition bonds	7	66	27
Sustainability-linked bonds	12	62	26
Sustainability bonds	14	71	15
Social bonds	12	62	26

SDG = Sustainable Development Goal.
Source: Authors' compilation based on survey results.

a EUR500 million SDG bond with a 12-year maturity and a coupon rate of 1.3% on the global market in September 2021. The proceeds from the sale are being used to support three priority sectors: social protection, education, and health. SDG bonds are similar to GSS bonds whose use of proceeds further aligns with and contributes to specific SDGs.[7]

The interest of investors in sustainability bonds coincides with the recent expansion of the sustainability bond market in Indonesia, as their aggregate annual issuance volume in 2021 surpassed that of green bonds for the first time. According to the International Capital Market Association, sustainability bonds are bonds in which the proceeds are exclusively applied to

---

[7] ASEAN Capital Markets Forum. 2021. *ASEAN SDG Bond Toolkit*. Jakarta.

finance or refinance a combination of both green and social projects.[8]

Advisors, Underwriters, and Issuers

This section examines the interest of potential issuers of green bonds, the most promising economic sectors, and the various types of potential issuers from the perspectives of local advisors, underwriters, and potential issuers. From the perspective of advisors and underwriters, their clients are generally interested in and developing plans for the issuance of green bonds. It was encouraging to learn that all respondents indicated that their clients have some interest in issuing green bonds (**Figure 20**). However, issuers had an entirely different perspective. The majority of issuers indicated that they are not interested in issuing green bonds at this stage, which is greater than the percentage of issuers who are interested but lack the knowledge and resources to do so (**Figure 21**). A small proportion of respondents

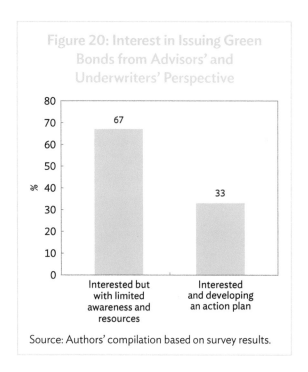

Figure 20: Interest in Issuing Green Bonds from Advisors' and Underwriters' Perspective

Source: Authors' compilation based on survey results.

indicated that they are interested in issuing and are developing an action plan. This demonstrates the need for listed companies to continue developing their green bond knowledge and resources.

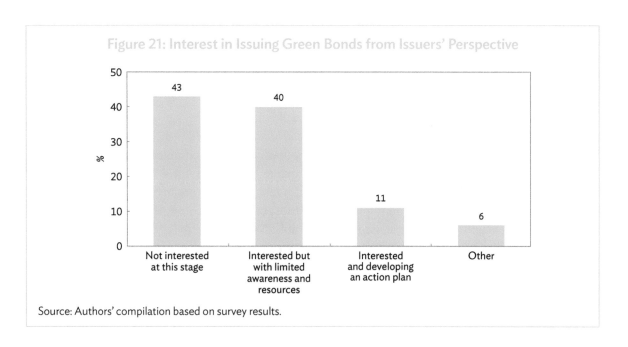

Figure 21: Interest in Issuing Green Bonds from Issuers' Perspective

Source: Authors' compilation based on survey results.

---

[8]   ICMA. 2021. *Sustainability Bond Guidelines*. Zurich.

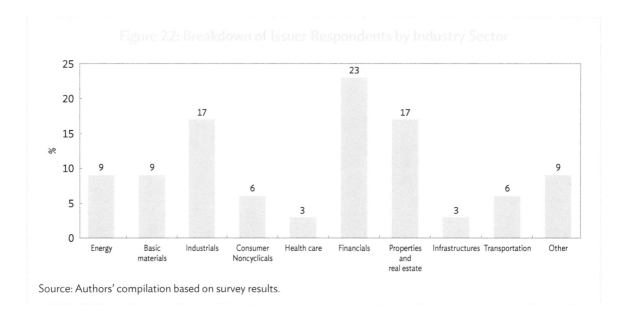

Figure 22: Breakdown of Issuer Respondents by Industry Sector

Source: Authors' compilation based on survey results.

More than 40% of the issuer respondents have a market capitalization of less than USD500 million, while 26% have a market capitalization of between USD500 million and USD2 billion. Only 3% of issuer respondents have a market capitalization of USD50 billion or above. The majority of issuers operate in the financial, real estate, and industrial sectors (**Figure 22**). There is relatively little representation from the energy, consumer, technology, and transport sectors.

In terms of issuance size, around 33% of advisors and underwriters indicated an optimal issuance size for green bonds greater than USD100 million, while another 33% of respondents shared that the optimal deal size should be less than USD10 million (**Figure 23**). Despite the fact that the majority of sustainable bonds from Indonesian issuers are denominated in US dollars, the majority of them had issue sizes in excess of USD100 million.

In terms of sectors, the majority of advisors and underwriters agreed that renewable energy presents the greatest opportunity for the issuance of green bonds in Indonesia over the next 3 years (**Figure 24**). Additionally,

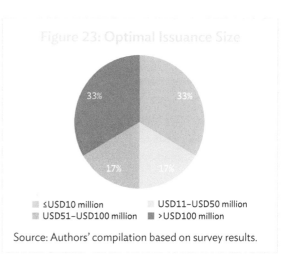

Figure 23: Optimal Issuance Size

- ≤USD10 million
- USD11–USD50 million
- USD51–USD100 million
- >USD100 million

Source: Authors' compilation based on survey results.

20% of respondents agreed that both green buildings and energy efficiency hold significant potential for the Indonesian green bond market's development. Although advisors and underwriters view green buildings as one of the most promising sectors, the sector comprises only 3% of the portfolios of local institutional investors and is not considered one of the most promising sectors from investors' perspective.

When asked why clients should issue green bonds, all advisors and underwriters cited the possibility of reduced funding costs. Approximately 67% of respondents believed this

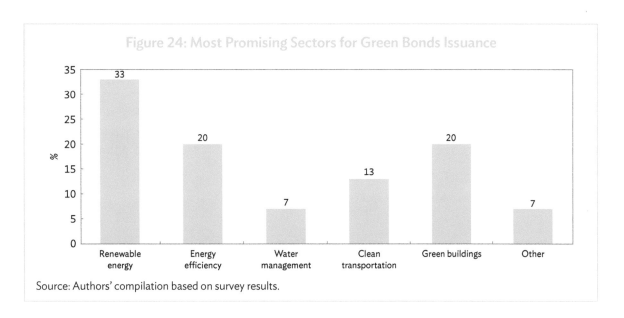

Figure 24: Most Promising Sectors for Green Bonds Issuance

Source: Authors' compilation based on survey results.

to be the most compelling reason for companies to issue green bonds, while 33% believed it to be a valid reason (**Figure 25**). For 50% of respondents, attracting new types of investors is the most important factor, while the remaining 50% considered this to be an important factor. All respondents believed that the issuance of green bonds would enhance an organization's green image and be a key motivator for issuers to integrate ESG into their corporate DNA.

Additionally, 83% of respondents agreed that green bonds could be issued in response to investor or lender demand.

Unlike advisors and underwriters, issuers believed that improving an organization's green image and enhancing the quality of corporate disclosure are two of the most important and relevant reasons for issuing green bonds. Additionally, issuers indicated that the ability

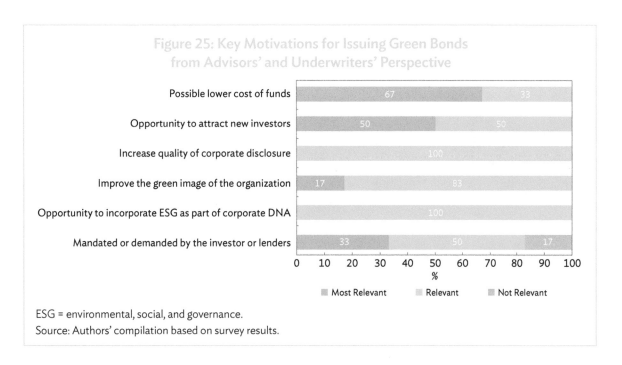

Figure 25: Key Motivations for Issuing Green Bonds from Advisors' and Underwriters' Perspective

ESG = environmental, social, and governance.
Source: Authors' compilation based on survey results.

to attract new investors is more important than the possibility of a reduction in financing costs (**Figure 26**).

Advisors and underwriters, as well as issuers, agreed that the lack of knowledge and awareness about green bonds is the most important

obstacle preventing them from issuing green bonds (**Figure 27** and **Figure 28**). Advisors and underwriters believe that the lack of clear benefits of green bonds over conventional bonds is the second most important factor, while issuers believe that the additional procedures and costs associated with the

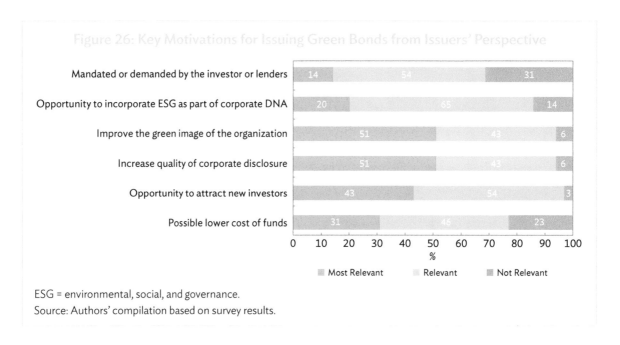

Figure 26: Key Motivations for Issuing Green Bonds from Issuers' Perspective

ESG = environmental, social, and governance.
Source: Authors' compilation based on survey results.

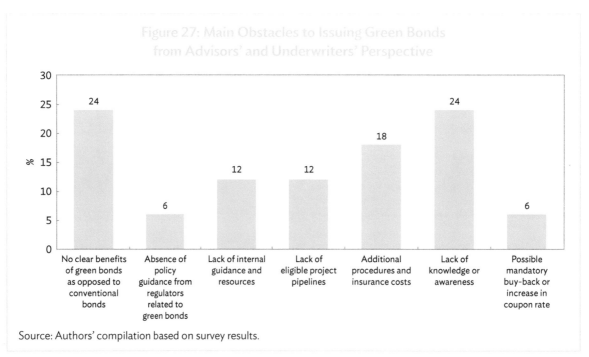

Figure 27: Main Obstacles to Issuing Green Bonds from Advisors' and Underwriters' Perspective

Source: Authors' compilation based on survey results.

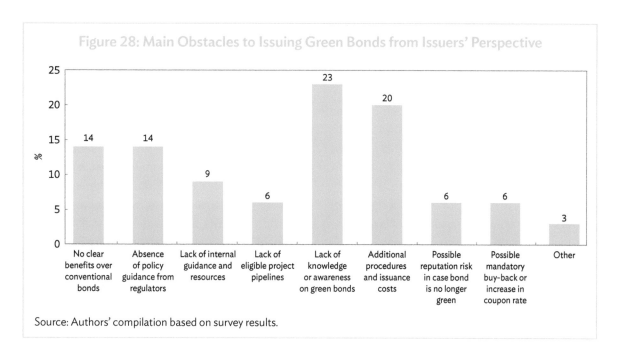

Figure 28: Main Obstacles to Issuing Green Bonds from Issuers' Perspective

Source: Authors' compilation based on survey results.

issuance of green bonds is the second most important obstacle. Interestingly, the absence of policy guidance from regulators was seen as less of an impediment from intermediaries' perspective. This demonstrates the strong leadership of the domestic regulator in implementing measures that have facilitated the emergence of the green bond market in Indonesia.

Respondents were then asked to identify key drivers that could increase green bond issuance in Indonesia. Local underwriters and issuers have differing perspectives. While underwriters indicated that increased investor demand is the most important factor to drive increased green bond issuance (**Figure 29**), the majority of issuer respondents indicated that tax incentives and/or government subsidies are the most

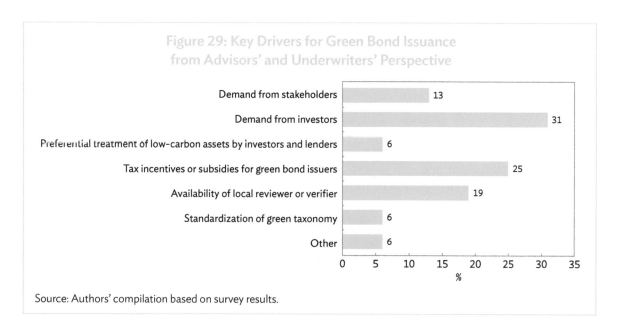

Figure 29: Key Drivers for Green Bond Issuance from Advisors' and Underwriters' Perspective

Source: Authors' compilation based on survey results.

important factor (**Figure 30**). A significant number of underwriters also indicated that tax incentives and subsidies are important.

Surprisingly, none of the underwriters indicated that promoting ESG reporting on stock exchanges would be relevant to increasing green bond issuances in Indonesia, despite the fact that approximately 14% of issuer respondents indicated that this is one of the most significant drivers. Contrary to the responses of issuers, the majority of underwriters believe that the availability of a local reviewer or verifier is the most important factor.

When asked about potential investors in green bonds, all respondents believed that development partners could significantly contribute to the growth of the local green bond market by investing in green bonds issued by their clients. Meanwhile, all respondents agreed that development banks, the social security fund, and commercial banks should invest in green bonds, with nearly 50% believing that insurance companies, pension funds, and asset managers could also play a significant role in facilitating the issuance of longer-term debt (**Figure 31**).

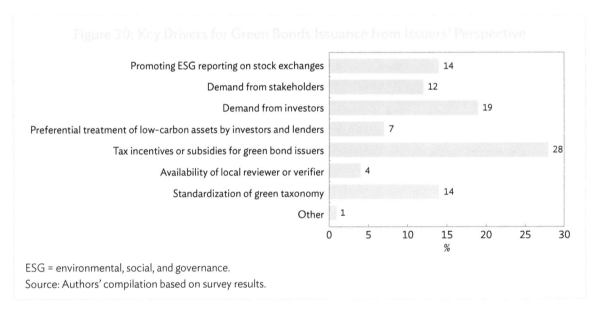

Figure 30: Key Drivers for Green Bonds Issuance from Issuers' Perspective

ESG = environmental, social, and governance.
Source: Authors' compilation based on survey results.

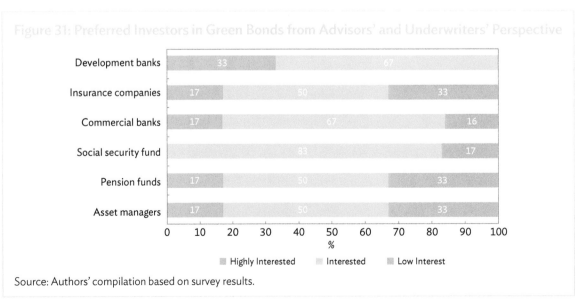

Figure 31: Preferred Investors in Green Bonds from Advisors' and Underwriters' Perspective

Source: Authors' compilation based on survey results.

Advisors and underwriters, as well as issuers, were asked about policy options that could be implemented to support the development of the Indonesian green bond market. Contrary to institutional investors, underwriters and advisors believe that an increase in the pipeline of eligible projects for green bond issuance and preferential purchasing from central banks, pension funds, and insurance companies are required to further develop Indonesia's green bond market (**Figure 32**). This is in contrast to investors, who gave less importance to these two policy options. In addition, clear green definitions, a streamlined cross-border fundraising framework, and making green bonds the default option for new pension fund account holders were of importance to advisors and underwriters.

Issuers indicated that tax incentives for green bond issuers and investors would be the most effective policy option for promoting the market. Consistent with the perspective of local advisors and underwriters, issuers also believe that clear policy options from the government and clear green definitions are beneficial. Importantly, all issuer respondents indicated that having a centralized platform that provides information

on all sustainable bonds issued by Indonesian entities and an expanded green project pipeline are crucial for making issuance decisions (**Figure 33**).

In terms of capacity building, a majority of advisors and underwriters believe that investors and asset managers would benefit the most from training to help them better understand green bonds and why they should include them in their investment strategy (**Figure 34**). All respondents also believed that board members of state-owned enterprises and the teams inside investment banks and securities firms closing deals should be trained to help increase the supply of green bonds. Indeed, 33% of respondents believe that training for these two groups of stakeholders is critical, while 67% believe it is necessary. This demonstrates that state-owned enterprises could play a leading role in proving their environmental and social commitments and assisting Indonesia in reaching its net-zero emissions goal by 2060 through the issuance of green bonds. All respondents agreed that chief financial officers of large corporations and listed companies require training as well.

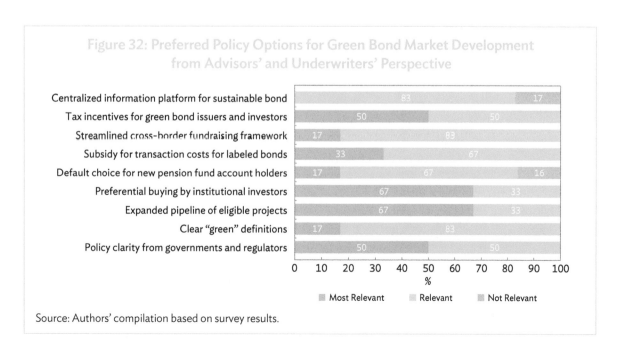

Figure 32: Preferred Policy Options for Green Bond Market Development from Advisors' and Underwriters' Perspective

Source: Authors' compilation based on survey results.

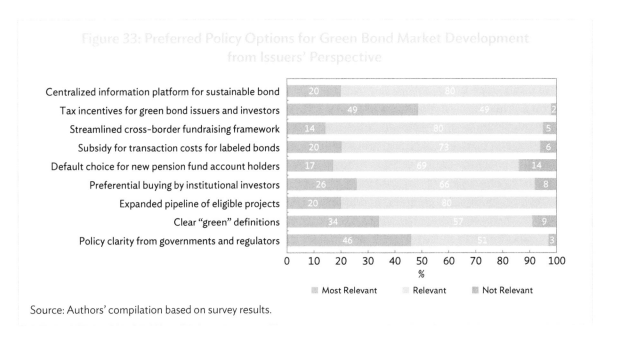

Figure 33: Preferred Policy Options for Green Bond Market Development from Issuers' Perspective

	Most Relevant	Relevant	Not Relevant
Centralized information platform for sustainable bond	20	80	
Tax incentives for green bond issuers and investors	49	49	2
Streamlined cross-border fundraising framework	14	80	5
Subsidy for transaction costs for labeled bonds	20	73	6
Default choice for new pension fund account holders	17	69	14
Preferential buying by institutional investors	26	66	8
Expanded pipeline of eligible projects	20	80	
Clear "green" definitions	34	57	9
Policy clarity from governments and regulators	46	51	3

Source: Authors' compilation based on survey results.

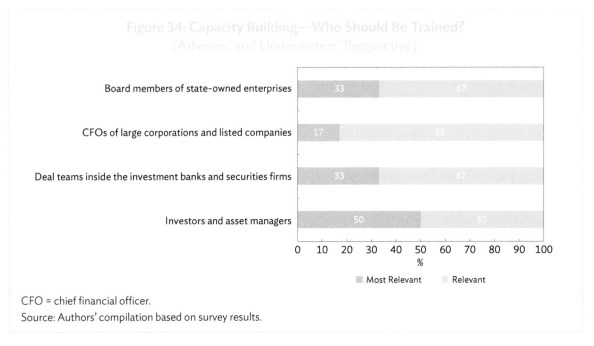

Figure 34: Capacity Building—Who Should Be Trained?
(Advisors' and Underwriters' Perspective)

	Most Relevant	Relevant
Board members of state-owned enterprises	33	67
CFOs of large corporations and listed companies	17	83
Deal teams inside the investment banks and securities firms	33	67
Investors and asset managers	50	50

CFO = chief financial officer.
Source: Authors' compilation based on survey results.

Similarly, the majority of issuers believe that institutional investors should be trained on the importance of ESG investments. As issuers, chief financial officers of large companies should be trained so that ESG considerations can be incorporated into their financing strategies. Similarly, deal teams and underwriters need a deeper understanding of green bond issuance processes in order to better advise clients (**Figure 35**).

Lastly, advisors, underwriters, and issuers were asked about their interest in other sustainable finance instruments that could help mainstream climate finance to support sustainable bond market development in Indonesia (**Figure 36**). The majority of underwriters believe that sustainability bonds and sustainability-linked bonds are the two instruments with the most potential impact.

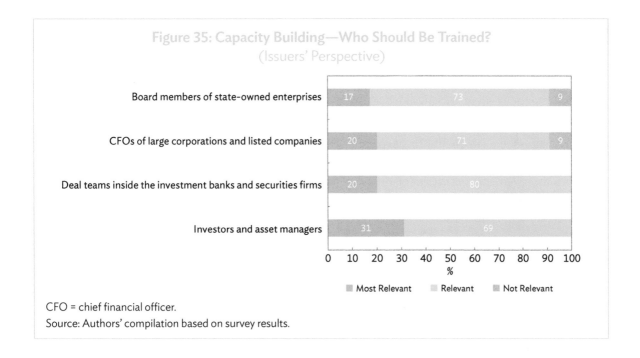

Figure 35: Capacity Building—Who Should Be Trained?
(Issuers' Perspective)

CFO = chief financial officer.
Source: Authors' compilation based on survey results.

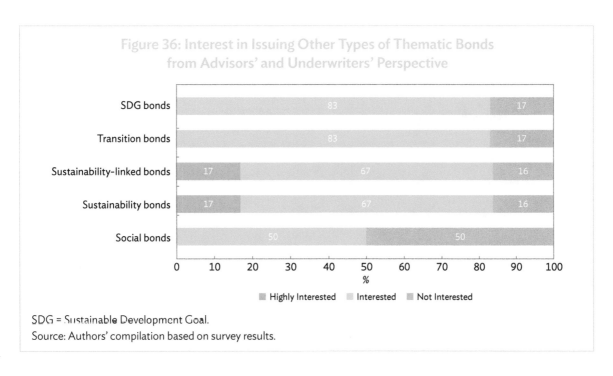

Figure 36: Interest in Issuing Other Types of Thematic Bonds
from Advisors' and Underwriters' Perspective

SDG = Sustainable Development Goal.
Source: Authors' compilation based on survey results.

According to the International Capital Market Association, sustainability-linked bonds are any type of debt instrument for which the financial and/or structural characteristics can vary depending on whether the issuer achieves predefined sustainability or ESG objectives. In that sense, issuers are committing explicitly (including in the bond documentation) to future improvements in sustainability outcome(s) within a predefined timeline. Sustainability-linked bonds are a forward-looking, performance-based instrument.[9]

Meanwhile, a majority of issuers are interested in exploring sustainability and transition bonds (**Figure 37**). Transition bonds refer to instruments that are used to fund activities that are not either low- or zero-carbon emissions but that can play a short- or long-term role in decarbonizing an activity or assisting an issuer in transitioning to compliance with the Paris Agreement.[10]

Similar to the responses of advisors and underwriters, less interest is shown in social bonds due to their restricted use of proceeds for social projects. Issuers may prefer to issue sustainability bonds where bond proceeds can be allocated to both green and social projects, making the issuance size more feasible from a bond issuance standpoint and allowing for more flexible use of proceeds from the issuer's perspective.

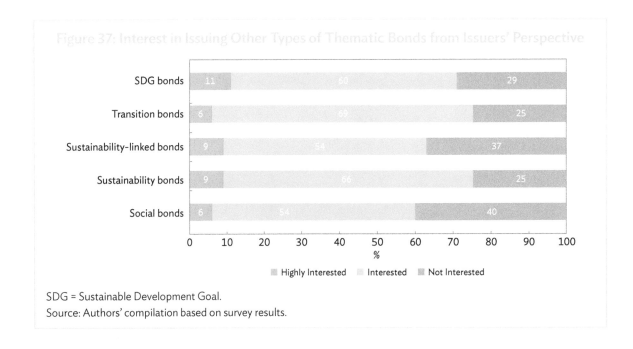

Figure 37: Interest in Issuing Other Types of Thematic Bonds from Issuers' Perspective

SDG = Sustainable Development Goal.
Source: Authors' compilation based on survey results.

---

9   ICMA. 2020. *Sustainability-Linked Bond Principles.* Zurich.
10   ADB. 2022. *Promoting Local Currency Sustainable Finance in ASEAN.* Manila.

WHAT ADB CAN DO TO HELP

Respondents identified several ways in which ADB can assist the Indonesian green bond market's development. These beneficial recommendations can be classified as follows.

As a Knowledge Partner

ADB could provide knowledge support to relevant stakeholders in Indonesia, including potential issuers, capital market intermediaries, institutional investors, and the general public. This is particularly relevant, as many stakeholders have indicated that their lack of awareness is an impediment to more green finance.

ADB can collaborate with a development partner such as UNDP to provide technical assistance to relevant stakeholders in Indonesia (**Box 3**). For example, to facilitate the development of the green bond market in Indonesia, ADB can encourage financial market authorities to provide relevant frameworks and standards and make it easier for stakeholders to evaluate green bonds and their associated benefits. The more successful examples of green bond issuance will trigger other companies to follow suit in using green bonds as an alternative source of funding and at the same time help combat the impact of climate change. Also, ADB can provide some capacity building support to help develop a risk management framework for the banking, asset management, and insurance industries and risk-based supervision guidelines for supervisors in the context of implementing climate-related

financial risks to enable issuers to improve their disclosure practices.

ADB could also assist in providing updates on the development of the sustainable bond market via *AsianBondsOnline*. This would increase market participants' awareness of such instruments and increase the knowledge of financial practitioners.

As an Investor, Issuer, and Guarantor

Development partners like ADB could act as anchor investor to increase demand for green bonds and as an advisor for global green investors to invest in Indonesia's green bonds. ADB can help to enhance the credit rating of the issuer through its trust fund, the Credit Guarantee and Investment Facility. Doing so would result in a lower cost of capital for Indonesian companies since more investors would be interested in such investments. Moreover, ADB can boost investor confidence in green bonds, signaling to the market that they are investment-worthy opportunities. The increase in demand for green bonds would also encourage more issuance of green bonds in the country.

ADB can support the development of the green bond market in Indonesia by facilitating loans for financially sustainable infrastructure projects and local companies in Indonesia through a wider network channel and encouraging more

Box 3: ADB's and United Nations Development Programme's Technical Assistance to Potential Indonesian Issuers

The Asian Development Bank (ADB) is implementing a regional technical assistance (TA) program to develop an ecosystem for sustainable local currency bond market development in the Association of Southeast Asian Nations (ASEAN) plus the People's Republic of China, Japan, and the Republic of Korea—a grouping collectively known as ASEAN+3. Under the guidance of ASEAN+3 finance ministers and central bank governors, this TA was developed and implemented in accordance with the ASEAN+3 Asian Bond Markets Initiative's (ABMI) Medium-Term Road Map for 2019–2022. As a result, this TA program is truly owned by ASEAN+3 governments.

The project provides end-to-end support to sustainable bond issuers to ensure successful bond issuance, from project selection to development of a sustainable bond framework and engagement of external review providers. The project has recently supported several sustainable bond issuers in the region such as Thailand's Central Pattana Plc. Group, Government Savings Bank, and Thaifoods Group.

Meanwhile, the United Nations Development Programme (UNDP), under its Innovative Financing Lab, continues to take an active role in supporting the development and deployment of innovative debt instruments and mechanisms for the attainment of the Sustainable Development Goals (SDGs) by domestic stakeholders. This is fulfilled through the provision of TA to potential issuers, both in the public and private sectors, throughout the cycle of thematic bonds. TA is provided throughout the pre-issuance phase in the development of appropriate thematic frameworks as well as the project evaluation and selection process—ensuring their alignment with existing market principles and standards as well as the SDGs. The support carries over to the post-issuance phase with the bond's impact measurement and reporting process.

ADB and UNDP would be happy to provide consultation and technical hands-on support to Indonesian companies wishing to issue green, social, sustainability, and/or SDG bonds in Indonesia.

Source: ADB and UNDP.

banks and financial institutions to issue green bonds. In addition, ADB can help raise awareness of the negative impacts of climate change and inform investors of the increased risks posed by climate change impacts. Also, ADB can support the establishment of an independent agency to provide second-party opinions, limited assurance, and rating and scoring for green and ESG investments.

Finally, ADB can support the financing of green projects by acting as a "first-loss" investor in pooled investment vehicles that aggregate smaller projects, helping to attract private investors to invest in senior layers of the capital structure. By bringing its expertise and capital to such deals, ADB can help scale up the market effectively.

FINAL WORD FROM SURVEY RESPONDENTS

Survey respondents were asked to give some final words on green bond market development in Indonesia. The following list comprises a few highlight responses:

Supply

- The green bond market's development will need support from the government. Green bonds should offer competitive interest rates for investors.
- The Government of Indonesia needs to develop more green projects in collaboration with the private sector.
- Green bonds in Indonesia should be denominated in rupiah and have a lower interest rate. They should be supported by the Government of Indonesia with a tax deduction or tax holiday.
- There should be a law or OJK regulation requiring institutional investors to allocate a certain portion of their portfolios to green assets.
- An eligible green project pipeline is needed in Indonesia. There is a lack of awareness of green instruments among bond market participants.
- The supply of and demand for green bonds exists, but investing in them has not yet become a necessity in the market.

Demand

- The green bond market in Indonesia is still very limited in terms of instruments, so it has considerable potential to be developed in Indonesia.
- Green bonds in Indonesia will grow rapidly in line with the government's commitment to reduce greenhouse emissions by 41% by 2030.
- Green bonds can be an investment alternative for bond investors seeking to diversify their portfolio.
- Relevant stakeholders need to work together to increase green bond issuances in Indonesia, which will provide greater investment options for investors.
- If the regulator allows investment outside of Indonesia, we would also buy ASEAN green bonds.
- Green bonds are a perfect match for long-term investments such as pension fund.
- It is important to measure the impact of climate change on financial markets in Indonesia.
- Many Indonesian investors, especially retail investors, only pay attention to returns and are not paying much attention to environmental aspects. This is a challenge for the development of a green bond market in Indonesia.
- Most investors still see green bonds from the commercial side (i.e., coupon rate), yet there is no coupon compensation on the "green" label. Issuers need incentives

for the additional costs (e.g., second opinion) of issuing a green bond. On the other hand, investors need a push to purchase green bonds (e.g., mandatory green asset allocation or a tax benefit).

Market Development

- The awareness of green and sustainable investments is improving in our country. The OJK regulations regarding sustainable finance have encouraged issuers to apply sustainability and green aspects in their business activities. The success of sovereign sustainable bond and green *sukuk* issuances has attracted global green investors to our country, contributing to momentum among all stakeholders toward developing a green and sustainable bond market in our country.
- Policy mechanisms that would increase green bond issuance include tax incentives and subsidies for green bond issuers, tax incentives for the coupon received by green bond investors, more incentives from the regulator, and a policy from the regulator mandating a certain percentage of ESG investments for institutional investors.
- Sustainable economic opportunities remain high along with already strong regulations in the market. Meanwhile, Indonesia has adopted a sustainable economic growth approach via Law No. 16/2016 Concerning the Ratification of the Paris Agreement. The OJK also issues various regulations, including OJK Regulation No. 51/2017 Concern ing the Implementation of Sustainable Finance for Financial Service Institutions, Issuers, and Public Companies.

- There are exciting opportunities for Indonesia to develop and add inventory to the green and sustainable bond market, which needs more support from the government in terms of incentives, socialization, and a roadmap for both issuers and investors. As investors globally have put more importance on and targeted exposure to this type of investment, quickly developing the Indonesia green bond market could attract more potential investors.
- Indonesia needs more time to educate investors and potential issuers.
- At this stage, the green bond market is not yet attractive due to the lack of guidance, resources, and regulation.
- Clear guidelines and incentives from the government is necessary. Meanwhile, issuers should put in place a mechanism to ensure that environmental objectives are achieved as intended following the allocation of bond proceeds.
- A local environmental expert who can provide green bond verification services would be extremely useful.
- The proliferation of standards, frameworks, and guidelines—as well as the diversity of market practices in terms of definitions and requirements for green bonds—create complexity and confusion among issuers and investors.
- A standardized taxonomy and disclosures for green bonds is necessary, including having an external reviewer for green labeling, as well as enhanced information on green bonds via common bond platforms.
- We need to work together to expedite the practice of sustainable finance for future generations.

NEXT STEPS

This survey found that the majority of investors, advisors, and underwriters, as well as issuers, are committed to becoming more environmentally friendly in terms of both investment and fundraising. However, there are a significant number of respondents that are not yet interested in investing or issuing green bonds at this stage, while others are interested but do not have sufficient capacity to seriously look into these instruments. As a result, development partners, in collaboration with relevant regulators, can play a key role in strengthening the capacity of local capital market stakeholders, as well as issuers, to mainstream climate finance and expand both the eligible project pipeline and the issuer base.

Currently, the Indonesia green bond market is dominated by three sectors: renewable energy, energy efficiency, and clean transportation. It is critical to further diversify and identify potential issuers from other promising sectors—such as sustainable agriculture, water and waste management, and green buildings—to provide them with more funding opportunities and to give investors more investment opportunities.

As Secretariat of the ABMI, ADB will continue to work closely with local regulatory bodies and development partners to establish and strengthen the ecosystem necessary for the Indonesian sustainable finance market's development, including capacity building, publication of guidance notes and handbooks, and technical assistance to issuers on their sustainable finance journey.

CPSIA information can be obtained
at www.ICGtesting.com
Printed in the USA
LVHW071057210223
739960LV00023B/1831